Purpose. Passion. People.

*A 30-day devotional to activate your purpose
and build your personal brand*

Glynis L. Jones

Purpose. Passion. People.
A 30-day devotional to activate your purpose
and build your personal brand

ISBN 9798711957294

Dedicated to:

The one who was "an inspiration to all,"
love and miss you Daddy

My heartbeats RCJIII, CRJ, CAJ

foreword

Purpose, passion, and people – the 3 Ps of life. Passion is what fuels everything. It's what motivates and drives us. Passion is what shapes your purpose in life and in business. The success of our passion depends on the people we partner with and, the people we surround ourselves with. It takes a team of people who share a vision, a dream, and goals in order for a business, and to a certain extent – our individual lives, to reach full potential.

If you don't know your purpose, you can't execute your passion. As a result, you won't be able to clearly communicate your drive, your motivation, and your "why". When you're not operating in your purpose, it is all too easy to veer off of your path and it's extremely difficult to maintain inspiration. When this happens, it becomes challenging to find your calling and to build a culture of authenticity and passion that resonates with others.

This book is a collection of daily devotions that will challenge and motivate you to the next level. As a faith-filled woman of God, my sister G. Lynn is an inspirer. Inspiration is part of her DNA! Our father instilled in us the will to be an inspiration to all. G. Lynn has a way of bringing purpose to life. When everyone else views a simple picture as black and white, she sees the splash of red, a dot of yellow, multiple lines of green, various shades of blue, and a blotch of orange. Through her creative and artistic lens, she has a way of bringing to life everything she touches. As you read these daily devotions, view it through the eyes of the author. Let this book come to life in you. Don't only read the devotions, but apply them to every area of your life. Be ready. The best is yet to come!

Carmen M. Elliott, MS, CAE

contents

introduction

What is the connection between purpose and personal branding?

For a little background information - the idea of personal branding started with an article by Tom Peters in Fast Company magazine (1997) *"A Brand Called You."* Tom Peters said *"All of us need to understand the importance of branding. We are CEOs of our own companies: Me, Inc. To be in business today, our most important job is to be head marketer for the brand called You."* Since then, this idea has blossomed and of course is now a concept that you hear often.

I have been building my personal brand for almost 10 years now. I had originally positioned myself as a designer, doing small projects for different people. However, I soon realized that I needed to take a step back, to strategize and understand the value of a brand before creating all of the artful brand elements. Since I've made the decision to help businesses and individuals creatively convey their message and build thriving brands, I've had the opportunity to work with both small and large organizations, as well as individuals. However, I still know there is more to come. We all have to start somewhere, and that is why I am so passionate about working with people like you that know they have a seed that needs to be nurtured and watered.

Your brand is your reputation. What do you

want to be known for? Before you say, "I don't care what people think about me," stop...because you do to some extent. When you go into an interview, you care what the interviewers think of your presentation and whether you had more to offer than the other candidate. When you engage in public speaking, you care if the participants are listening and receiving what you have to share. We may say we don't care, but we have to in order to improve. That's how we get better. Even Jesus had a reputation. His name and His amazing works and teachings preceded Him.

I think where we can get lost in the personal branding space, is when we're so invested in what people think of us that we try to change who we are. I want to help you view personal branding through the lens of fulfilling your purpose and being who God created you to be.

Before we were conceived – God had a purpose for our lives. (Jeremiah 1:4–8)

God knew the day we would be born, and from that day forward we were on our paths to fulfilling our purpose for Him. My philosophy is as follows:

Personal branding is putting your purpose into action.

I'm sure you're asking yourself: *"How is this devotional even going to work? Where in the Bible does it talk about having a personal brand...and where is she even going with this? How is she going to connect scripture and branding?"* Well, let me ask you this – **does the Bible talk about purpose?** Of course it does!

I want to help you remove the superficial ideas of personal branding, and instead view it as a mechanism to mobilize the gifts and talents that God has blessed you with. It's an avenue to impact people and to make your mark in the world.

I created this book because I believe in purpose and I know the power of commitment. I'm convinced that we all have an assignment in life. As a branding and marketing professional, I appreciate the value in packaging what you know and sharing it with others. Given the access to information through social media and the Internet, I also appreciate the importance of providing tools to help you control the narrative of your brand.

You need the cornerstones: purpose, passion, and people. These three work together and intersect; in the center is where you will find the sweet spot, Your Personal Brand. In 30 days we will focus on five core sections **Prayer, Purpose, Passion, People and Personal.** These sections support the framework for building a strong personal brand. Within each section you will find scriptures and messages to meditate on. I've also included some nuggets from my own personal experiences - as a reminder that you're not on this path alone. Each day with this devotional we are building and growing together. Be sure to make a move every day, to take action to activate your purpose. Now, let's begin this personal brand journey and dive into the first section.

prayer

Let's set the stage for everything with Prayer. *Prayer is powerful* and it will help you hone in on your purpose. Prayer is a tool we can all use to have a personal conversation with God. When you talk to Him, you can also hear from Him about the direction for your life and specifically your personal brand. The messages in this section will help you use prayer to support your personal branding roadmap.

day 1

Meditate on this:
For God has not given us a spirit of fear but of power and love and a sound mind. –2 Timothy 1:7

Message for the day:
Step out on faith with your idea.

Has God given you numerous ideas? This is probably one of the reasons that you decided to pick up this book and have an interest in building your brand. Most likely, you have notebooks, sticky notes or Word and Google documents full of different ideas that have come to you in the middle of the night or even while you were driving. Unfortunately, for some of us, those ideas never leave the paper, because we haven't created a plan or we haven't moved forward to implement them. Why is this, is it fear? Is it procrastination?

It's not enough to simply pray for a plan; we have to continue to pray and activate our faith to put our plan into action. Building a brand, promoting a book, accepting your first speaking engagement or launching a business can be scary and intimidating. Fear may take over you and make you believe that it's not your time. Trust me when I tell you that there is someone out there waiting for what you have to offer.

I remember when I hit send on the email that helped launch my brand almost 10 years ago. It was actually on my birthday, and the same day that I announced to my husband that we were expecting our first child. Can you imagine the range of emotions I was feeling on that day? I was nervous, I was anxious, I was excited, but I also wondered how I would be received. Would people want to do business with me? Would they perceive the information I had to offer to be helpful or of any use?

It was at that moment that God reminded me, He blessed me with gifts and power! He had blessed me with my unborn son, a true gift and with the ability to move forward with my business. Today's scripture always comes to my mind if I'm feeling fearful about how and when to move forward.

Make a move:

You know you need to take the next steps to move forward, but what is holding you back? Whatever it is, write it out, meditate on today's scripture, pray about it, and then take the first step to MOVE!

notes

Meditate on this:
And the Lord answered me, and said Write the vision and make it plain upon tablets, that he may run that readeth it. –Habakkuk 2:2

Message for the day:
Pray for a plan.

All businesses, non-profits, educational institutions and churches, have some form of a vision statement. A vision statement is a clear, aspirational declaration that helps guide the focus, the decisions, and the work of the organization. As we build our personal brands, it's imperative that we also develop a vision statement to help guide the plan for our brand. This scripture is the epitome of having faith in your ideas.

I've written out the vision for my brand and how it will ultimately support my business. I've also developed a detailed business plan and I continue to expand it. You must pray and seek God for a plan for your brand. Ask God what you need to do to build it. He will reveal the plan to you in various ways. This makes me think of another scripture; *Commit thy works unto the Lord, and thy thoughts shall be established (Proverbs 16:3).*

He will allow you to read articles that may spark ideas, or align you with someone to have a conversation, resulting in you having a different and new perspective about your original ideas. We can make a plan but how that plan will be implemented is really up to God and His divine will for our lives. All of this is easier said than done, but I've found comfort in knowing that if I just give it to God, He will ensure that the plan is successful. If you have the vision, God will provide the provision.

Make a move:
Have you written out your vision statement? Try writing it out today.

What does your brand plan look like? Meditate on the scripture – just as God spoke to Habakkuk, He will help bring your plan to fruition.

notes

day 3

Meditate on this:
And Moses answered and said, But, behold, they will not believe me, nor hearken unto my voice: for they will say, The Lord had not appeared unto thee. –Exodus 4:1

Message for the day:
Pray for message clarity.

One of the keys to having a strong personal brand is having a clear and concise message. You can make a great impact if you know what you're saying and who you are saying it to. A clear message will resonate with whomever it is intended for. Moses had a lot of excuses about why he couldn't speak out and share the message of God with the Children of Israel. You know, we can probably get away with using excuses on some people, but God is not here for our excuses. He has equipped you with everything you need. Moses tried many excuses - but there was a calling on his life and an assignment to fulfill. For every excuse he tried to give, God responded with a solution.

To be honest, there was a point in my journey when my messaging was all over the place, and I thought my target audience was "everybody." I really had to pray and consider who needed to hear what

I had to say, where was the need, and who could I help with my services? My old friend, Doubt, tried to creep in and make me believe that maybe what I had to say wasn't important or relevant. However, God wouldn't let me use that excuse. As you can see, I am writing this book. These words are meant for YOU. Yes you. I believe that the blueprint offered in this devotional will help as you build your personal brand. Remember, God has given YOU a purpose AND a voice for a reason.

Make a move:
Think about who you want to connect with through your brand. Who can benefit from what you have to share?

Now, consider your core messages. Write down three core messages that you believe are foundational for your personal brand.

notes

Meditate on this:
Joshua told the people, "Consecrate yourselves, for tomorrow the Lord will do amazing things among you." -Joshua 3:5

Message for the day:
Pray, and then get ready to pivot and proceed.

Joshua is one of my favorite leaders in the Bible. His obedience to God and implementation of strategic direction is an excellent example of how we can exemplify leadership, which is a critical component of a strong personal brand. In this scripture, Joshua was preparing the Israelites to cross the Jordan River. Joshua guided the Israelites along the way, but now they were preparing to do something that only God could help them do.

As I'm writing this book, the world is experiencing a global pandemic. There have been stay-at-home orders placed across the nation. Many are practicing social distancing, businesses deemed non-essential have been closed, and many children are learning from home. The new state of affairs has impacted many businesses and brands. There has been and continues to be a lot of transition. In times like these, it's important to be ready to pivot. We are experiencing something that only God can bring us out of.

As you build your brand, you will experience roadblocks, like the rivers of Jordan and the walls of Jericho. There may be times when you just don't know what to do next. However, whatever the situation, I encourage you to pray for direction. Where would God have you to go next on your brand journey? Some doors may close, but others may open and you should position yourself so that you are ready to walk through them.

Make a move:

Are you stuck? Do you only see the Jordan ahead of you? Know that God has given you an opportunity to use your voice that could transform a program, your community, or even the world!

Write down one challenge you're currently facing in your personal brand journey.

Take time to pray, and meditate and know that God is willing and able to help you pivot and proceed.

notes

day 5

Meditate on this:
Very early in the morning, while it was still dark, Jesus got up, left the house and went off to a solitary place, where He prayed. –Mark 1:35

Message for the day:
Pray for peace.

Self-care is important. Starting out the day with prayer, meditation and scripture is important for maintaining self-care and keeping your peace. We see in this scripture, that even Jesus needed some space and quiet time for prayer. In the verses before this, Jesus traveled to heal the sick, cast out devils, and minister to others. Jesus was putting in the work! I am definitely not comparing our efforts to Jesus, but we do work hard! Some of us are running businesses and households; others are leaders and executives in our career fields. We are working diligently every day to hone our crafts. But beware, sometimes we get so caught up in being busy that we lose sight of our goals, our purpose and our assignment. Our busyness can cause us to be overwhelmed and lead to stress.

Stress can take you out! Stress can manifest in the body in so many different ways. It can impact you mentally and physically. I've personally witnessed this with my husband, he will have to write his own book to share his testimony. But with prayer and seeking direction from God, he was healed and his peace was restored.

This is why we need to pray for peace, because life will throw some curve balls your way. God gives us that peace that passes all understanding. Practicing self-care and self-awareness will allow you to connect and go deeper into prayer, and it will help you block out distractions so that you can focus and reconnect with yourself, and most importantly, with God. You must be grounded and in a good place in order to be a blessing to others. Your mental, physical and spiritual wellness all contribute to your core being, so take care of yourself.

Make a move:
Find a quiet place for your prayer time. For some it's in the car. For others it's in the office. Some even have it in the bathroom or closet. Wherever it is, choose a place where you can have peace and quiet from all distractions, and you can pray for strength and direction.

notes

purpose

We've set the atmosphere with Prayer, now let's move on to *Purpose, the core of our personal brands.* Sometimes we go through life wondering, what is our true purpose, why are we here? This section will affirm that you were created for a specific purpose and will give you guidance on how to activate your purpose to build your brand.

day 6

Meditate on this:
A man's gift maketh room for him, and bringeth him before great men. –Proverbs 18:16

Message for the day:
Be authentic.

God has placed something original inside each one of us. Does it ever blow your mind to think that you are the only person like yourself in this world? Sure, there may be someone out there who shares your name or looks similar to you (shout out to the look-alikes out there). Maybe you even get the comment, "You know...you look so familiar." In addition to God making us all unique, He has also placed something inside of us. We all have a purpose in life, and it's up to us, with God's guidance, to work towards fulfilling our purpose daily.

One of the keys to a successful and thriving personal brand is authenticity – being who God made you to be. It's easy to look at others and marvel at what they are offering, but you have your own story to tell. You are unique and it's those unique attributes that help build trust for your brand. When I first started my venture into personal branding and wanted to consult with individuals, there was one particular personal branding coach that I followed. I read all of her blogs, and the emails from her list. I also attended one of her in-person trainings. I thought she was absolutely amazing, but I had to come to the realization that I couldn't be like her. I couldn't deliver content the way she did. I had to do it my own way. I had to be ME. I had to share my own story.

God has given you a gift - and the scripture tells us that our gifts will make room for us. Understand that your gift is going to be your platform and it's your unique ability that is going to help your brand thrive. Your gifts are going to open doors. Your gifts will put you in conversations, and have you seated at tables that you never thought you could come to.

Make a move:
Don't squander your gift. Recognize the gift and the purpose that God has blessed you with.

Write down at least one gift that makes you unique.

Ask a few trusted sources what they see as your unique gifts and what they have noticed that makes you truly excited.

notes

day 7

Meditate on this:
For we are his workmanship, created in Christ Jesus unto good works, which God hath before ordained that we should walk in them. –Ephesians 2:10

Message for the day:
Carry on with your purpose and your calling. You were built for this.

Have you ever tried to give up? I mean, like really decided you were done. You were so done that you slammed the laptop closed, you tossed the drawings, you pushed the books across the table and then folded up your arms and pouted. I'm with you, I've been there. There have been times when I was totally through with this idea of building a brand and a thriving business, but God wouldn't let me throw in the towel that easily.

You see, if we give up, we are basically saying, "I don't trust you God, or the plans that you have for me." It's kind of rude to tell the Creator that you don't trust Him. There is an old saying that says, "God doesn't make junk." The scripture lets us know, we are His "workmanship," created by Him and for Him. So, guess what? NO! You can't give up today or ever.

You must continue to do the work. Building your personal brand will amplify your value to the world; it will operationalize your purpose, it will allow others to experience what God has made so that He can get the glory!

Make a move:
We're not pouting today. We're actually about to go harder. Take it up a notch by identifying one task that you've been working on for your brand. Then go all the way in!

notes

day 8

Meditate on this:

*13 Let me tell you why you are here. You're here to be
salt-seasoning that brings out the God-flavors of this
earth. If you lose your saltiness, how will people taste
godliness? You've lost your usefulness and will end up in
the garbage. 14 Here's another way to put it: You're here
to be light, bringing out the God-colors in the world.
–Matthew 5:13–14*

Message for the day:

What's your personal brand mission statement?

I absolutely love The Message Bible's
interpretation of this scripture. Feel free to read the
King James Version if you need less sass and color in
your scripture! But the way it starts off, "Let me tell you
why you are here…." How many of us sometimes have
asked ourselves that question, "Why am I here Lord?"
He tells us in the scripture, we are the season salt (yes,
I flipped it), to bring out the God-flavors of the earth.
Salt or NaCl is an essential mineral substance – WE
are essential. The scripture doesn't stop there.

It goes on to tell us that we are "here to be a
light…bringing out the God-colors in the world." Don't
you love that? Doesn't that make you excited about
your purpose and what you've been called to do?

That is why you have to activate your purpose and share it with the world. Organizations, businesses and brands have crafted mission statements to share their purpose with the world. Guess what? You need to do the same for your personal brand.

Tell folks who you are and what you have to offer. Think about your skills and abilities, and consider your personality traits and operation strategies. Don't forget your values, dreams and passions and why you do what you do. All of this contributes to your personal brand, and provide insight to craft a clear and concise brand mission statement. Here, let me share my statement:

> *My mission is to use my passion for people and purpose as well as my expertise in branding, marketing and management to inspire women to activate their purpose and develop their personal brands.*

Simple enough, right? Now you try.

Make a move:
If you don't already have one, develop a personal brand mission statement. It should be concise, but informative. You should be able to clearly and concisely state your mission, if you are ever asked about it. Here's a framework to help:

> *My mission is to use my [skills or expertise] to inspire/ lead [group of people] so that [ultimate goal].*

*Note: The mission statement is not the same as your vision statement. Remember, earlier I mentioned the vision statement. They are definitely two different concepts.

notes

Meditate on this:

And whatever you do, do it heartily, as to the Lord and not to men. –Colossians 3:23

Message for the day:

Operate in excellence.

Always demonstrate consistency and quality. In other words, bring your A+ game at all times. I know this already sounds exhausting, but how you handle your brand is a reflection of you. I'm not making this stuff up. Even the scripture says to do it heartily (e.g., entirely, totally, completely, genuinely, warmly). We have to give our best and in an orderly manner.

This is why I want to focus on your organizational and management skills. There are aspects of building and maintaining a personal brand that may be difficult, but there are also tools and resources in place to help you manage your brand. You can use a project management tool like Asana, or create a Google document or spreadsheet to assist with tasks, such as tracking deliverable due dates, scheduling upcoming speaking engagements and monitoring the status of guest-writing assignments.

I know this sounds like a lot. Don't worry though. You're on your way to having an assistant that can take care of all of this for you. In the meantime, being organized will help you to stay consistent with your brand and offer quality to your audience.

Make a move:

While we're activating our purpose, we must remember that this is our brand, and anything we put out there is a direct reflection of ourselves. Get organized. Organization is an important component to make this thing work!

Identify an organizational system that works best for you: a planner, a calendar, or a project management tool. Choose a system and go to work!

notes

day 10

Meditate on this:
Being confident of this very thing, that He who has begun a good work in you will complete it until the day of Jesus Christ. –Philippians 1:6

Message for the day:
Be confident.

You have to believe in your ability and what you have to offer to the world. You know you're a rock star, right? But for some reason, feelings of self-doubt sneak up on you and at times you feel inadequate, this is called imposter syndrome. According to a review article published in the International Journal of Behavioral Science[1], at least 70% of people deal with imposter feelings at some point in their lives.

I confess, I am guilty of this myself. I know what I bring to the table, and I know what God has blessed me with, but there are times when I'm like, "What am I really doing?" These people have credentials, and double-digit years of experience. A little background for you, I've worked with researchers for most of my career. Individuals with several letters behind their names, that used sesquipedalian prose in regular lunch conversations, which may have required you to go to dictionary. com when you went back to your desk. Did you catch that?

Truth moment, I had a slight case of imposter syndrome when I started writing this book, but then today's scripture came to me. God gave me this assignment and I'm going to see it through and whoever this is for, they will receive it and apply it to their lives. You have to know that God is going to guide you.

Make a move:
Here we go. In what areas of your life do you lack confidence? Write them down.

How will this impact your brand?

What are you going to do to fix it? (Hint: Seek God first…)

notes

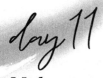
day 11

Meditate on this:

24 She maketh fine linen, and selleth it; and delivereth girdles unto the merchant. 25 Strength and honor are her clothing; and she shall rejoice in time to come.
–Proverbs 31:24-25

Message for the day:

How can you package your expertise?

What is it that people always come to you for? Do they invite you to speak on a specific topic? Do they ask you to give them advice on their outfit, or how to decorate their home? Maybe they ask you to review their social media or website content. Whatever "it" is, clearly, you're good at it because people are asking you to do it for them. Trust me, no one would ask if that wasn't your thing. This is your opportunity to package it and make it available to the world.

I know sometimes this can be intimidating, but you can start small. The Proverbs 31 woman made clothes for her family, and she then took that show on the road. She began making more clothing and selling it. Of course, the Proverbs 31 woman seemed to be great at *everything,* but she chose one of her many talents and built a brand on selling fine linen.

We all have to start somewhere. Why not start with our God-given talents?

Make a move:
What do you want to be known for?

What are you good at it? Does it solve a problem for people? BOOM, that's it! Write it out and brainstorm how you can bundle it and bless the world.

notes

passion

Priscilla Shirer shares in her book Fervent, *"Passion is the fuel in the engine* of your purpose. It's your "want-to". It's what keeps you going when mundane tasks bore you or difficult ones dissuade you. Passion is what keeps you moving in the direction your best intentions want to go."[2] Think about that definition as you read through this section. These messages will remind you to think about your "why," how to keep your "why" alive and how to communicate and share your "why" with others.

Meditate on this:
But seek ye first the kingdom of God, and his righteousness; and all these things shall be added unto you.
–Matthew 6:33

Message for the day:
What are you passionate about?

We should start here. What keeps you up at night, wakes you in the middle of the night, or wakes you early in the morning? Maybe it's the idea you continuously write about in your planner or jot down on those sticky notes, which are strategically placed around your office. It's the project that you're so over and think you can't go any further, *but* you remember your purpose and you keep going.

That's why I pulled this scripture. It's actually one of my favorites. When I lose the pep in my step or get fatigued as I continuously pursue my passion, I think about this verse. This scripture reminds me that I need to seek God *first;* the key word here is *first.* So that means that I don't go to Him after I've already mapped out the plan and implemented, but I go to Him first and then He will get things in order for me. He will give me the strength I need. Your passion is what is going to help your personal brand thrive. As the introduction said, your "passion is the fuel in your engine." When you partner your passion with your experience, you can create a killer brand.

Make a move:
Can you easily articulate what you're passionate about?

Take a minute to write it down, and if you've already done this; write it down again. Remember, your passion is what is going to keep you going when this thing gets hard.

notes

day 13

Meditate on this:
My sheep hear my voice, and I know them, and they follow me. –John 10:27

Message for the day:
What is your brand voice?

You know what you're passionate about, right? Whatever "it" is, it's going to keep your personal brand going. Now you need to think about the voice of your personal brand. Your brand voice should align with your brand values. Think about the tone of your brand; is it intellectual, fun, inspirational, motivational, educational, or authoritative? More importantly, how is it conveyed through your brand? Those who connect with you often will begin to know your brand voice and for your target audiences it should automatically resonate with them.

I would say my brand voice is inspirational, informative, motivational, conversational and nonjudgmental. My audience connects with my voice. Like this scripture, Jesus said that "my sheep," also known as His people, His following, they all hear His voice. They know the voice of the Lord, and He knows them; it all works together to build a relationship.

Make a move:
How can you convey your brand voice in your personal brand? Think about three ways you can ensure that your brand voice resonates with your audience.

notes

day 14

Meditate on this:
1 When Paul and his companions had passed through Amphipolis and Apollonia, they came to Thessalonica, where there was a Jewish synagogue. 2 As was his custom, Paul went into the synagogue, and on three Sabbath days he reasoned with them from the Scriptures, 3 explaining and proving that the Messiah had to suffer and rise from the dead. "This Jesus I am proclaiming to you is the Messiah," he said. –Acts 17:1–3

Message for the day:
Be strategic and position yourself as a thought leader.

When someone is passionate about something, they usually don't have a problem with speaking up and out about the specific topic. As you build your personal brand, it's important that you apply this same practice. Identifying opportunities to speak will help strategically position you as a thought leader in your field. Let's take a look at Paul in this scripture. Paul was very passionate about the message that he had to share, and also strategic about where he went to speak, to ensure that his message was heard.

I have a friend that is a professor, and she has taught public health courses for years both to undergraduate and graduate students. When she first started, she asked me to come and speak to her students about personal branding. Initially, I was wondering how is this going to work? I'm not a public health professional, how can I speak to them about personal branding?

However, after thinking more about the opportunity, the audience and the importance of personal branding, I was able to develop a signature session on Building your Public Health Brand. I've been speaking to her classes for several years now. Thanks to this opportunity, I've continued to stand out and position myself. Here's the thing, you're likely going to have to step outside of your comfort zone, but this is the only way you will grow. Seek out various speaking opportunities and be open to different platforms and audiences.

Make a move:
Public speaking is a critical element of your personal brand. Consider what speaking opportunities you would like to pursue.

Start to outline a signature talk that you can take on the road!

notes

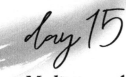
day 15

Meditate on this:
Study to show thyself approved unto God, a workman that needeth not to be ashamed, rightly dividing the word of truth. –2 Timothy 2:15

Message for the day:
Study your craft and read up on your industry.

Being passionate means that you have a strong belief or intense feeling about something. You are dedicated to understanding and learning about that something. I think back to when my husband was studying for his Information Technology certifications; there were flash cards and pre-tests, and somehow, I surprisingly found myself recruited for study sessions. I could probably tell you a little bit about security, risk management and network security. My point is, you have to study, and you have to take time to dig deep into your craft.

If you're going to position yourself as a thought leader around a particular topic, you have to know your stuff. In this scripture, the Apostle Paul was schooling Timothy, before his death (Paul). He is basically letting Timothy know he has to put in the time, so that he can be great, and deliver results that he will be proud of. Outside of our devotion time, sometimes it's just enough for us to make time to read through our emails; but we have to prioritize. You will have to find time to read an article, attend a workshop or conference, or download the latest e-book. If you're going to be the best, if you are the expert; then you will have to put in the work.

Make a move:
I challenge you to identify at least one workshop and/or conference per quarter. Don't ever think you are beyond learning something new. We should commit to being a life-long learner.

notes

Meditate on this:
Behold, I will do a new thing; now it shall spring forth; shall ye not know it? I will even make a way in the wilderness, and rivers in the desert. –Isaiah 43:19

Message for the day:
Think about the impact you are making or can make.

Your passion can make an impact. Through your speaking, writing, art, or any other craft you have mastered; you can influence others. You can influence decision makers, consumers, and mentees. It will take time to create an impactful and influential personal brand, but don't get weary as you continue on this journey. You will learn what resonates with your audience, and identify key attributes that distinguish you from others, including your competitors. These are all elements that will contribute to building an impactful personal brand.

Through your personal brand, you can offer new opportunities for an individual, an organization or for a group of people. This scripture reminds us of how God told the Israelites that He was going to do a new thing for them. Your impact can demonstrate a new experience or a new, creative way to do something. Never underestimate the power and the meaning of your brand. As you build your personal brand you will build your influence.

Make a move:
What does a successful, impactful and influential personal brand look like for you?

Think about what new thing you want to do. Write down at least 3 descriptions of "What does success look like to me?"

notes

day 17

Meditate on this:
1 Now when Jesus was born in Bethlehem of Judaea in the days of Herod the king, behold, there came wise men from the east to Jerusalem. 2 Saying, Where is he that is born King of the Jews? for we have seen his star in the east, and are come to worship him. 3 When Herod the king had heard these things, he was troubled, and all Jerusalem with him. –Matthew 2:1-3

Message for the day:
Word-of-mouth is a powerful promotional tool for your brand.

People need to have something to talk about, so give it to them! Here is your opportunity to apply your impact and share your passion. Word-of-mouth remains to be a proven marketing tactic. Think about how you may need a new stylist, or lawncare, or maybe a good tailor; you ask a friend or post on Facebook what you are looking for, and someone will share a referral. Usually, people share information about services that they've had a good experience with, and then you, in turn, may refer that same service to someone else; just passing along the information.

Many of my opportunities have come from

referrals, where someone heard that I consulted or provided specific services. I'm so grateful for those opportunities, but I was also mindful of my performance, because I want folks to continue to refer me and share their experiences.

The birth of Jesus was indeed something to talk about! This scripture is just one example of how word-of-mouth can work. Although the wise men were guided by the star, they helped start the conversation and communication about the King that was just born. When I think of word-of-mouth communication, I sometimes think of the game, Telephone. Do you remember that childhood game? The game would start with one person passing a message, and it would pass from person to person and by the time it got to the end, the message would be something totally different.

Your job is to ensure that what's said about you and your brand is consistent – you can help control this by personally sharing your story, by showing up and by speaking out. Give them something to talk about!

Make a move:
Control the narrative of your personal brand. Do a quick internet search of your name or business. What pops up? Does it align with your personal brand? If not, you have some homework to do.

notes

people

Where would we be without the people in our lives? There are those that are on our team, pushing us up the hill, and there are others that are waiting to see us fall. All of them, play a part in the success of our brands. Don't forget the people that you serve through your brand, your target audience, your consumers, constituents, and your community. ***People make the world go around!*** The messages in this section will help you take a closer look at the interpersonal aspects of brand building.

Meditate on this:
The blind receive their sight, and the lame walk, the lepers are cleansed, and the deaf hear, the dead are raised up, and the poor have the gospel preached to them. –Matthew 11:5

Message for the day:
Know your audience.

A thriving brand requires interaction. You will have to connect and engage with various people as you continue on this brand journey. It may be people like me who are here to help and consult with you along the way, or it may be people that will give you your next career opportunity. Maybe it could be people that provide funding and that want to invest in your passion project. You must also remember the people that you are trying to reach through your brand. Never underestimate the connection you make with people. Your connection has a purpose.

Knowing and understanding which group or groups of people need what you have to offer, and how it will help them is vital. Jesus was very aware of His audience. This scripture aligns with the time when Jesus was teaching and preaching in Galilee. Actually, this is His response to a little fact checking about who He was, and He simply affirmed those inquiries, and tells them to report what they've witnessed. He's basically saying "Hey, my work speaks for itself."

He knew that there would be naysayers, folks that were curious, and some who may have been confused. But most importantly, He knew there were people in need. There were people that needed His love; the blind, the lame, the diseased, the deaf and the poor. Jesus sets the example for ensuring that we are attuned to the needs of our audience.

Make a move:
Think about who's your target audience. Who are you trying to reach?

Create a target persona for your ideal consumer. Consider their demographic characteristics. Where do they live? Where do they work? How do they receive content and information?

notes

Meditate on this:

15 Then Esther told them to reply to Mordecai: 16 "Go, gather all the Jews who are present in [a]Shushan, and fast for me; neither eat nor drink for three days, night or day. My maids and I will fast likewise. And so, I will go to the king, which is against the law; and if I perish, I perish!" -Esther 4:15-16

Message for the day:
Content is King.

I'm sure you've heard the saying that "content is King"; meaning that your content is important and it reigns when it comes to connecting with people. Well, content is Queen in this book. I recently read an article in Forbes and it reinforced that content mainly centers around the customer, or your target audience (see previous passage). It went on to talk about how content attracts people and when created, it should be more about them (the people) than you.

You have to create content that appeals to your audience, and the best part of this is that content can come in so many different forms. This book is a form of content. The weekly emails you receive from the list you subscribed to, is a form of content. Your lesson plan, your workshop session, your podcast episodes; these are all forms of content.

I love the story of Queen Esther because it exemplifies how God can and will use ordinary people to accomplish extraordinary things. Queen Esther had an assignment from God and didn't even really know it until the message came from her cousin, Mordecai. Queen Esther used the power of connections and content to give guidance to her people and save them. She was thinking about her people and contemplating what she needed to do for them. Although she didn't feel comfortable and knew that it was a possibility that she could lose her life, she realized she had an assignment. Queen Esther gained favor with the King and positioned herself. Her message, her instructions, and her content was the beginning of the journey to fulfill her purpose.

Make a move:
When you are preparing content, think about how it can connect and resonate with your audience. Remember the end goal. What is the impact you want to make?

How can people benefit from the content you provide?

notes

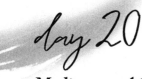
day 20

Meditate on this:
So, he cut two tablets of stone like the first ones. Then Moses rose early in the morning and went up Mount Sinai, as the Lord had commanded him; and he took in his hand the two tablets of stone. –Exodus 34:4

Message for the day:
You need a digital home.

Do you have a virtual storefront or a digital home to connect with people? I mentioned to you in the introduction of this book that you have to establish your brand before you get into the exciting artful elements like developing a logo, or building a website. Well, we've already discussed developing your core message, your mission and vision and now that you know who you're talking to, you should be in a good place to develop your brand website.

Your brand website is the digital headquarters where you can connect with your target audience; this is your platform and an opportunity to express your brand to the world.

A few things to consider for your website, the content should speak to your audience. This isn't the time to focus on how great you are; you should be highlighting how you can help your audience. Your greatness, however, shouldn't go totally unnoticed.

Present your greatness through your brand story. Telling your story will help you connect with your audience. Let them realize that you are a person too. You want to make sure that the look and feel of the design aligns with your brand. Don't forget images; you're going to need eye-catching high-quality photos to present your brand.

Lastly, what do you want your website visitors to do? You must include a clear call to action on your website. You have their attention, so let's give them something to do!

Now, you read this message and then you went back up to the scripture to try to connect the dots, right? Let me share my train of thought about this. Moses didn't have WordPress, Squarespace, Wix or Weebly, but he had two stone tablets that he used to write the words of the covenant – the Ten Commandments. I imagine that those stone tablets weren't painted and embellished with diamonds, but that they were sturdy and large enough so the people way in the back could see them. Know that God will use different mechanisms and channels (like your website) to make sure the message is reaching the people.

Make a move:
If you don't already have a website, start putting a plan into place. Think back to your core messages, and what content you want to share. Most importantly consider the best platform for you and your budget.

notes

Meditate on this:

11 And He gave some, apostles; and some, prophets; and some, evangelists; and some, pastors and teachers; 12 For the perfecting of the saints, for the work of the ministry, for the edifying of the body of Christ. –Ephesians 4:11-12

Message for the day:

Customer service is paramount.

Who doesn't appreciate good customer service? I always tease my sister, because she is that person that will write a letter or send an email if and when she receives bad customer service. But I get it, when you make an investment, you expect a certain level of service. Trust me, the follow-up emails, handwritten notes, quick texts to touch base, and phone calls along the way can make a significant difference in your customer relations. Going beyond that, true customer care can evolve service transactions into lasting relationships.

Take your customer service to the next level and send something special for your customer's birthdays or for key observances and holidays. It's all about building a relationship and rapport with your customers. You want them to know you are someone they can trust and rely on. You want them to feel special. You want them to come back. You want them to invite you to speak at multiple events. You want them to place multiple orders. It always makes me smile when I get those emails or texts from clients that say "I appreciate you." That lets me know that I must be doing something right.

The roles listed in the scripture are positions that conduct works of service for the body of Christ. Putting in the extra work is critical. If you say you provide a specific service, put in the work and follow through. I realize this message may not apply to everyone right now, but you can simply consider your customer to be anyone who is consuming your content.

Make a move:
Think about the consumers of your content. People want interaction. What customer service do you offer them?

Do you respond to letters, emails, direct messages and comments in a timely manner?

Are there additional ways you can show true customer care?

notes

day 22

Meditate on this:
11 As iron sharpens iron, so a man sharpens the countenance of his friend. –Proverbs 27:17

Message for the day:
Who's in your tribe?

In order for your brand to thrive you will need to align yourself with like-minded people. We often hear the saying "iron sharpens iron," and it's a true statement. Surround yourself with other dynamic individuals who are interested in using their powers for good. I remember when I first started out and I would go to networking events for women business owners. Here I was with just a few projects under my belt, thinking I was going to go into this networking event and show off, and realized I was right where I needed to be.

It's the old saying, "If you're the smartest one in the room, you're in the wrong room." I needed to interact with these women who had successfully built their brands. I could learn from them and that was okay. It was at these events where I was able to identify a mentor and connect with other women who I could call for advice when I found it necessary. It was also at these events that I made connections for future partnerships.

Even when I think about my current circle of friends; I am surrounded by amazing women who are each making moves and thriving. Some have Ph.D.'s, others are creative and caring mothers; actresses, vice presidents, marketing executives, or engineers. You name it, they are all rocking it out! They continuously challenge me to do and be better, and I love it. Don't try to be in competition with your tribe. They are there to support you (and check you sometimes if needed and vice-versa; it's a two-way thing).

Make a move:
Make a list of your tribe. Next to each person's name write one word that describes their contribution.

Do they help foster a supportive or toxic environment?

Don't be afraid to distance yourself from the toxicity. Remember iron sharpens iron.

notes

day 23

Meditate on this:

16 Now as he walked by the sea of Galilee, he saw Simon and Andrew his brother casting a net into the sea: for they were fishers. 17 And Jesus said unto them, Come ye after me, and I will make you to become fishers of men. 18 And straightway they forsook their nets, and followed him. 19 And when he had gone a little farther thence, he saw James the son of Zebedee, and John his brother, who also were in the ship mending their nets. 20 And straightway he called them: and they left their father Zebedee in the ship with the hired servants, and went after him. –Mark 1:16–20

Message for the day:

Find someone who can help you.

I'm going to let you in on a little secret, you don't have to build your brand all on your own. God blessed other people with special skills and talents, just like He blessed you. Years ago I redesigned one of the many iterations of my website on my own. I was proud of my limited WordPress skills, but then the website began to malfunction and I really needed to enhance the features. I decided I couldn't do it by myself, so I went out on a limb and decided to find some help. I didn't have a huge budget, but I realized that I needed someone else with specific expertise.

After some research on a website that matches those in need of various services with local professionals, I made the investment, and I found an amazing web designer. She is a female business owner; whom might I add, I still work with to this day.

Jesus had help. He designated His disciples to be His hands and feet while He was on earth and when He left the earth. Jesus identified people that were strangers to be a part of His support system. As a matter of fact, He recruited them right off of their job sites. He knew the type of people He would need to assist Him in the ministry. Remember, a good team can help make your brand journey go a little smoother.

Make a move:
You know the gaps you have; you know in what areas you may fall short. Write down insights or skills you lack but know you will need.

Now identify names to write next to those things. If you don't know anyone personally, ask around within your network for recommendations.

notes

personal

There are two words in the term Personal Brand. Personal is the adjective or descriptor for brand, and it is a very important element. We often hear the phrase *"don't take it personal"*, but when it comes to crafting and building your own brand, you must take *all* of it personal. Every part of your ***brand needs to align with who you are as an individual;*** resulting in an authentic brand. The messages in this section will help you think about key factors that make you unique and ensure your brand is specific to you and that it reflects who you are and what you're about.

Meditate on this:

For do I now persuade men, or God? or do I seek to please men? For if I yet pleased men, I should not be the servant of Christ. -Matthew 11:5

Message for the day:

Social media is a digital self-representation.

Nearly 50% of the world's population (3.8 billion people) uses social media daily[3]. When used properly and positively, social media can have a great impact on your personal brand. The various platforms of social media offer additional channels to communicate your brand's message. However, you have to remember that your social media profiles are also a digital representation of yourself, so it matters what you say, what you post, and what you tweet and retweet.

Try not to get overwhelmed with social media; like feeling the need to be on every platform or posting all day, every day. Think about your audience and where they are. Are they on LinkedIn instead of Facebook? Maybe your brand is more visual and you need to leverage the photo and video sharing features of Instagram.

This scripture made me check myself and also

really think about how I use social media. In it, Paul is talking about preaching the Gospel, and takes a second to check things. He's like "Hold up, who are we trying to impress here as we share the Gospel?" It's not about pleasing people but making sure we are sharing what is right, and to ultimately please God. If nothing else, I think this scripture sets an example of how we too need to check ourselves and make sure that we are using these channels for the right reasons.

I will admit, I have a love/hate relationship with social media. I see how powerful it is, and that's just it, it is powerful. Social media can have an impact on your mental health, as you infinitely scroll and view others' lives; well, the parts that they want you to see. There have been times when I've had to take a social media fast. Basically, I took some time off of social media for a few weeks and I filled that time with reading and writing; other productive activities.

Too much of anything is not good for you, right? I guess my best guidance here is to use discretion, and use the channels in moderation. Regular engagement on these channels can support positioning you as a thought leader in your field, so be strategic in how you utilize them.

Make a move:

Do your homework and identify which social media platform is best for your brand.

Write down at least 2-3 key goals for the platforms you decide to use for your brand.

notes

Meditate on this:
I will praise You, for I am fearfully and wonderfully made; Marvelous are Your works, and that my soul knows very well. –Psalm 139:14

Message for the day:
Capture your greatness.

What do your headshots or brand photos look like? Headshots are also a form of self-representation, but through photography. "A picture is worth a thousand words" is what they say. With that being said, your headshots should speak for themselves. If your personal brand is bold, confident and dynamic, that should be conveyed through your photos. Maybe your personal brand is more creative, fun, and funky, and that can also shine through in a photo. Having at least one good headshot in your personal brand arsenal is critical. I believe in annually updating your headshots, to keep it fresh.

Remember you are fearfully and wonderfully made. Let that shine through your photos. Smile bright, let your eyes twinkle, and let others see your greatness. I remember when I first started consulting, having headshots was one very necessary investment. Looking back at those photos I see how my brand has evolved and grown. In those photos, I was younger. I seemed eager and confident in my abilities. Now viewing my photos several years later, that confidence is still there, but now I'm older, bolder and wiser.

Make a move:

Do you need headshots, or maybe you just need an update to reflect the current state of your personal brand? In either case, make sure you have your headshot and biography locked and loaded, and ready to share for your next opportunity.

notes

day 26

Meditate on this:

*12 And God said, this is the token of the covenant,
which I make between me and you and every living
creature that is with you, for perpetual generations: 13 I
do set my bow in the cloud, and it shall be for a token of
a covenant between me and the earth. –Genesis 9:12-13*

Message for the day:

Develop brand elements.

Don't you love to see a rainbow or even a
double rainbow after a storm has ended? When I
see a rainbow, I think of peace and comfort, but the
scripture reminds us that the rainbow represents
God's covenant with earth. There are several other
"symbols" throughout the bible. What does the
dove symbolize? What about a cross, what does
that represent? Do you see where I'm going with
this? These are all elements that convey a message
when you see them. In some way, they resonate
with individuals and have a specific meaning.

As you are building your personal brand,
you may decide to develop brand elements as
its representation. These elements may include a
logo, or type treatment of your name, a specific
color palette and possibly distinct fonts. My brand

elements have evolved over the years. If I had made the decision to include visuals in this book you could see how I transitioned from a boxy, brown and turquoise icon to a more simplistic turquoise circle with a white "G" in the middle. The "G" inside the circle represents so much for me; it represents wholeness, and a brand that is all encompassing. I've toyed with the idea of enhancing it, but I believe as my brand evolves so will my brand elements. However, I have made little additions like, adding to the color palette to allow for more flexibility.

Do what works best for you. Even if you have something in place now, it is okay to make changes or enhancements. The main goal is to have brand elements that accurately represent your brand and that are visually engaging.

Make a move:

Think about your brand elements and what they should represent. Write down ideas for your logo/type treatment and color palette that align with what you represent. It's okay if your brand evolves throughout your career.

Remember your brand is not just a logo or tagline or even a website; these are simply elements that support your brand.

notes

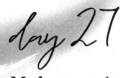
day 27

Meditate on this:
Let your light so shine before men, that they may see your good works, and glorify your Father, which is in heaven. –Matthew 5:16

Message for the day:
Never dim your light, people are watching.

Hey listen, this is your time to shine. One of the benefits of building a personal brand is that it gives you the opportunity to share with the world what God has blessed you with and how God is continuing to bless you. However, you should be mindful that with your light shining so bright, people are watching. Your light attracts people. They see your light; they notice that there is something special about you! This is why it is so important to be mindful of your attitude, your demeanor and your body language. Do these things align with your personal brand? I have to check myself on my facial expressions, because I sometimes have difficulty controlling them. The thoughts I have in my mind are immediately reflected through my face. I'm working on this, pray for me!

Today's message is inspired by a little

note that I received from a summer intern. I had been working with her on a few projects and had the opportunity to conduct a personal branding workshop with all of the summer interns. I love pouring into young people. I'm always encouraged by their potential. On the last day of the project, this young intern gave me a thank you note. It was simple and sweet:

"Thank you for introducing me to the ability and knowledge to brand myself. I really admire how you carry yourself and hope to learn from you! Wishing you the very best and to stay in touch. Sincerely, The Intern."

The intern's note was a reminder to me that I can never, nor should I ever dim my light, because others are watching. Her note also aligns with this scripture so beautifully. The scripture instructs us to let our light shine so they can see our good works. But, the most important part of this scripture is that this is done so that God can get the glory.

Make a move:
Do you always let your light shine? I know there are times when it's difficult, but I challenge you to always be aware of your attitude, your demeanor and your body language. Remember someone is observing.

notes

day 28

Meditate on this:
I can do all things through Christ who strengthens me.
-Philippians 4:13

Message for the day:
Practice your elevator pitch.

"What do you do?" How often do we hear
this question? This is when you shoot your shot
and whip out your polished elevator pitch, right?
We can always freshen up our pitch by adding
a few enhancements. I say enhance because we
grow, things change and we may want to highlight
something new that we have in the queue.

You should always be prepared to deliver your
pitch, you don't want to look like a deer caught in
headlights when you're asked the magical question.
Don't be nervous, think about the scripture. You
can do *all* things; you can even confidently chat it
up with the stranger you just met or the potential
employer, client or investor that has approached you.

Sometimes it's worth taking time to practice
so that it becomes second nature for you. Your
elevator pitch is part of who you are, and should
easily roll off the tongue. Also remember to keep
it brief, this is not the time to share your life story,

although you may get to that if a deeper discussion is warranted. Lastly, be easy with your delivery. Let it flow. It's a conversation, so you don't need to rush. You want the person on the other side of the conversation to hear everything that you have to say. As a child my mother would always tell me to **speak loudly, clearly and slowly,** and I use that until this day. *Thanks Mom!* Now, I'm sharing it with you, take your time and do your thing!

Make a move:

Can you share with someone in 30 seconds, who you are and what you do?

Can they get the vibe of your personal brand in that time?

Start practicing your elevator pitch today and remember to close the conversation with the opportunity or possibility to reconnect, if that's what you want.

notes

Meditate on this:
Come and listen, all you who fear God, and I will tell you what he did for me. –Psalm 66:16

Message for the day:
Tell your story.

Every morning I wake up thinking about my father. My father passed away from a heart attack when I was 8 years old. Although I was young I have so many great memories. I realize how much of an impact he had on my life even in those short 8 years. His presence in my life has really helped shape me into the person I am today. It's because of my father's love, guidance and the example that he set, that I do what I do. At a young age, he made me realize that I had purpose and that I had potential.

One Sunday morning my father told me that I was going to sing a solo in church, can you imagine the terror I felt as a 6-year-old standing in front of the congregation? But my father practiced with me, he played the piano and I sang my song. Another day, he told me that I was going to try out for the little league baseball team; again, big eyes, because I didn't think I could play, much less make the team. But my father practiced with me in the backyard, and then took me to the tryouts. Guess what? I made the team, although the smallest teammate, I made it! My father would never have the chance to attend any of my games as the spring season began, but his love and presence was felt.

My father believed in ME, and continued to inspire and encourage me even when I didn't believe in myself. This is why I have faith in true purpose and the power of personal brands. My father's purpose was to be an inspiration, to support others and help them believe in themselves.

I also believe in the power of sharing your story. The stories in your life have shaped you to be who you are. Don't be afraid to share your stories, they have helped you to build this authentic personal brand. The psalmist in this scripture is inviting others to come and hear his story, his testimony. He wants others to know what God did for him, so that maybe He can do the same for them. He wasn't ashamed to share how God had answered his prayers. We never know how our story may impact or help someone else.

Make a move:
What is your story? Remember your story is a part of who you are; it is what makes your personal brand unique and authentic.

Identify a way to weave your story into your personal brand so that it can accurately reflect who you are.

notes

day 30

Meditate on this:
For many are called, but few are chosen. –Matthew 22:14

Message for the day:
Put your purpose into action.

This is the last message for this devotional, and I feel it's important that I reflect on the words in the introduction. I created this book because I believe in purpose and I know the power of dedication. I believe that we all have an assignment. I hope this book has helped you to remove the superficial ideas of personal branding, and you can now view it as a mechanism to mobilize your gifts and the talents that God has blessed you with. Remember, it's an avenue to impact people and to make your mark in the world.

You've been called _and_ chosen to do something great in your life, I truly believe that. I believe this because you took the chance to pick up this book and with that, you obviously also realize the power and importance of commitment and the need to invest in your personal brand.

This is not a complicated concept. You are simply putting your purpose into action. You are packaging it in many different ways and sharing it.

Whatever the purpose is that God has placed inside of you, it's yours and yours alone.

Make a move:

Never forget your assignment and what you've been called to do. Never give up and remember you have to put in the work to get the results you seek.

notes

a note for you...

Dear Friend,

I thank God for you. I know it was the divine order of God that led you to purchase this book. I want to remind you that God loves you! Actually, He is crazy about you. He's so crazy about you, He sent His only son Jesus Christ to die for you! What a sacrifice. My prayer is that if you don't know Him personally, I welcome you today to begin your journey and amazing relationship with Jesus and accept Him as your Savior. I mean really, where else can you find a love like this?

Guess what else? I love you too and I hope you have felt the love in this book, even through the lens of building your personal brand. My desire is that you have been blessed by the messages that you've read and that you realize that God indeed has a purpose for your life.

Now go and be great!

Glynis

references

Sakulku, J. (2011). The Impostor Phenomenon. *International Journal of Behavioral Science*, 6(1), 75-97. https://so06.tci-thaijo.org/index.php/IJBS/article/view/521

Passion
Shirer, P. (2015). Fervent: A Woman's Battle Plan for Serious, Specific, and Strategic Prayer. Nashville, TN.:B&H Publishing Group

Personal: Day 24
Hootsuite.com (2020). Digital 2020: Social media use spans almost half global population. Retrieved from https://www.globenewswire.com/news-release/2020/01/30/1977203/0/en/Digital-2020-Social-media-use-spans-almost-half-global-population.html

Made in the USA
Middletown, DE
28 March 2021